WHAT EVERY TEACHER SHOULD KNOW ABOUT FINDING A JOB

A BEGINNING TEACHER'S HANDBOOK

Your Guide to Lifetime Earnings Exceeding $400,000

By

PHILLIP CARL SNYDER, Ph. D.

Boston
BRANDEN PRESS
Publishers

This book is dedicated to my wife
Jo Anna Summers Snyder
with continuing devotion and love

CONTENTS

PREFACE

What college doesn't teach you about earning a living as a professional educator

Today more and more college graduates are finding it increasingly difficult to search out and secure a teaching position in public education. This book is dedicated to the practical efforts and needs of those young people. The author realizes fully the discouraging aspects of spending $10,000 over a four-year period of one's life to complete a college education, which in our society is a symbol of success, and then only to find oneself unemployed. Within the context of this book you will find valuable information which will aid you in identifying and making application and eventually securing a position in the teaching field. One must always keep in mind that, although the formula presented here for successfully finding a teaching position is not infallible, the suggestions will undoubtedly contribute to a more expeditious and efficient process of applications and position selection. The format of the book is uncomplex and the information is explained in a logical, straightforward manner designed to convince—not confuse—the reader with regard to how to find a teaching job.

Once again as a beginning teacher, you must realize that your college education alone does not guarantee employment. It only guarantees that you have completed a required preliminary obstacle course which in some way or another is construed by our society to mean that you are prepared to carry out a certain function called teaching. This book explains explicitly how you take advantage of that experience and education and turn it into a profitable lifetime occupation. If this volume contributes to your gaining a teaching position, it will be well worth the effort required by you to understand its contents.

CHAPTER I

HOW TO APPLY

CAMPUS INTERVIEWS. In recent years campus interviewing has become more and more popular among public school systems. The reason for this increased interest in seeking out teachers from college campuses is obvious and logical. If school systems go to campuses, they have their choice of the cream of the crop in terms of teacher prospects for the coming year. Therefore, the campus interview is a very important aspect of finding a job as a teacher. A candidate looking for a teaching position should interview with as many school systems as possible and on a regularly scheduled basis as far as six months preceding graduation. The purpose of interviewing so often with so many systems is twofold: (1) It allows the interviewee an opportunity to develop his skills in the interview situation and increase his experience in dealing with interviewers with different approaches. (2) It allows you, as a prospective teacher, to establish yourself with many school districts, giving you exposure to potential positions which could possibly open later during the year. This provides you with built-in insurance that, if the position you desire first does not materialize, due to your interview exposure on campus you will probably be offered at least some position before the school year begins in September.

OFFICIAL TRANSCRIPTS. Official transcripts of college records are usually issued by the registrar's office. In some colleges and universities the college placement office also has copies of official transcripts. The official transcript is an important document in obtaining a teaching position. It provides the prospective employer with a record of your courses and professional preparation. You should make available to any employer you are considering a complete official copy of your transcript as soon as it is available after graduation. Although some universities charge a fee for providing transcripts, it is important that you incur the necessary expense to provide each employer a copy of

5

this transcript as soon as possible. The justification for this position is very simple. If the employer does not have a copy of your complete official transcript, it is impossible for him to hire you into the school system.

CREDENTIALS. Today every college has space set aside for a college placement office. The primary concern of the placement office is to develop a set of teaching credentials including reference sheets from college professors, records of student teaching, and recommendations from critic teachers and college supervisors, designed to present a positive image of the applicant to any school system. It is to your great advantage to have your credentials and the papers required by your placement office filled out completely and correctly and available when the campus interviews take place. Take time to do a careful job of filling out placement papers. This is one place where you can gain an advantage over many applicants for teaching positions. For example, I recall many misspellings on teaching placement service credentials. One that comes to mind involved a boy who listed chess as his major hobby; however, he spelled the word "chest." Remember that college recruiters are trained professionals. They have been recruiting in most cases for many years and have developed the ability to analyze credentials very quickly and thoroughly. When they read your credentials, what they see is what they know about you. If you make mistakes in spelling and grammar in preparing your credentials, these mistakes will surely be noticed and made record of by the interviewer. Your placement office credentials, along with many other elements of your personality, go together to make up your image as a prospective teacher. Do your very best to ensure that these records reflect your most credible assets.

PLACEMENT SERVICES. The college or university placement office is where your search for a position should begin. Usually there is a small fee connected with the service. For this fee you receive the use of the professional library which lists all positions presently open to the students of that particular placement office. You also receive a monthly listing of all positions in your area of interest and preparation. If you desire, you may arrange for counseling services from the placement office and, in many cases, detailed information concerning openings in particular areas of the country or school districts. Interviews are arranged for prospective teacher candidates and these are organized by the placement office. However, by far the most important service of the placement office is to develop a complete and accurate set of your teaching credentials and keep them on file for you for the remainder of your professional life. Without this service it is impossible for you as a professional to present an unbias opinion of your abilities to a prospective employer. Today, with competition for teaching positions at an all-time high, it is increasingly important that you have an affiliation with a teacher placement service and that you keep your records with that service up-to-date and available for use at your discretion.

WHAT RECRUITERS SEARCH FOR. All recruiters are searching for the overall image that a prospective teacher projects. That image consists of your transcripts from the college, credentials from the placement bureau, state certification as required by a state or local area, and your personal attitude, philosophy, and appearance at the time of the interview. Since many of these items are subjective, depending upon the individual recruiter and his opinions, it is to the advantage of the interviewee to analyze psychologically as much as possible the person who is interviewing him. For example, if the interviewer is dressed conservatively, and when you ask him questions concerning the school district and its program, his answers convey conservative ideas, it is to your advantage to observe this and make an effort to answer questions in a relative philosophical position. The interview is not a place to exhibit your individuality. It is a place to develop an understanding of the school system and the elements that the school system requires a prospective teacher to possess. The recruiter is the key. If you are applying for a teaching position in a school system with a dress code for students, then it would not be advisable for you to arrive at the interview with long hair, facial hair, or outlandish, unusual dress. This is not to say that in some school systems extraordinary appearance is not acceptable. For example, if you are applying for a teaching position in Harlem, or another large metropolitan system, few restrictions would be placed upon you with regard to your physical appearance. If on the other hand, you are applying in a very conservative school district in southeastern Ohio, it would be much to your advantage to take this into consideration when appearing for the interview. In other words, let your conscience be your guide, but don't be naive as to the effect your image will have upon your acceptability as a prospective teacher for that school system.

Recruiters are very much interested in what you have to offer the school system in terms of professional ability. Therefore, you should stress any special abilities you feel you possess as a teacher. If you are a particularly good disciplinarian, indicate this. If you have new ideas of methods of presenting some particular aspect of your subject matter, don't hesitate to share these with the recruiter. On the other hand, be prepared to admit your weakness as a prospective teacher. If you have had difficulties in the past, allow the recruiter the element of honesty needed to share these weaknesses with him, without stressing them overtly. This will save you endless hours of suffering after you have accepted the position.

Recruiters have certain positions in mind when they are interviewing prospective teacher candidates. By discussing your strengths and weaknesses as a teacher with the interviewer you insure that he will at least consider you for an appropriate position. We would assume, of course, that your primary desire is to seek a position which will be satisfactory to you and not just a position for the sake of being employed. Most recruiters will also have certain questions that would like to cover with you. Normally these relate to such things as teaching methods, classroom discipline, student evaluation, your ability to organize and plan lessons, your ability to accept constructive criticism, your feelings toward administrative and Board of Education officials, and your interest in professional and teacher organizations. It is to your advantage to be honest and straightforward in your approach to these questions. Answer them to the best of your ability without revealing any excessive bias in any direction. This approach allows you the advantage of not only understanding better the situation which you are facing, but also allowing the recruiter to reserve judgment upon your position until you are better acquainted with what is expected of you as a prospective teacher in a particular school system.

THE IMPORTANCE OF THE INTERVIEW. The entire process of finding a teaching position can be compared very much with the process of marriage in our society. The courtship is represented by the campus interviews and the information gathering of transcripts and credentials. This is followed by the actual "ceremony," the entering into of the contract, which is then followed by a prolonged period of living together—the actual performance of the teaching function within the school system. Therefore, the importance of the interview if obvious.

Many school systems require two interviews completely independent of one another. For example, a prospective teacher might be interviewed on campus by a member of the administrative staff. After application is made to the school system, a record of that interview is kept for future reference. If a position opens in the applicant's field, the applicant is asked to come in for a second interview within the school system. This interview may be carried out by a central office personnel manager or in some cases the principal of the building in which the teacher will actually be working. No matter what the interviewing procedure is, the interview remains an important part of the total process of seeking a position. A candidate should always make every effort to present himself, his philosophy, and his particular point of view in a favorable light whenever he is faced with an interview situation. In most cases this requires preliminary preparation. Researching the school system for which you are making application is essential, as is psychologically analyzing at the time of the interview the desires of the interviewer in terms of the responsibilities expected by the applicant. If you, the prospective teacher, possess any strengths, these should be stressed in the preliminary interview, and every effort should be made to make a favorable impression upon the interviewer. Correct English usage, appropriate dress, appropriate attitude and philosophy are all important parts of the overall image that you project in the preliminary interview. If you

9

fail to capture the interest of the employer during the preliminary interview, your chances of eventually becoming employed by that school system are greatly diminished.

WHAT IS REQUIRED BEFORE YOU CAN BE EMPLOYED. Almost all school systems require completion of an application form. Along with the application there are three other customary demands: (1) Each applicant must submit a copy of his offical transcripts. (2) Each applicant must submit a complete set of his college placement credentials. (3) Each applicant must submit a copy of his state certification for teaching. Upon receipt of these three items, plus completion of at least one interview, any applicant is eligible for employment within a school district. You must meet these three requirements of the information gathering process before the officials of the school system may submit your name to the Board of Education for approval as a teacher in that system. Many applicants forfeit the possibility of an assignment on the basis of not providing the certification, credentials, or official transcript to the school system. Therefore, it is impossible for the school system to hire them whether or not they have a position available.

Providing copies of your complete credentials, transcripts, and certification could become a costly process. For example, if you apply to fifty different school systems and you submit to each the three items indicated plus postage and correspondence to accompany them, this could involve a considerable amount of money. I feel it is important to mention that this is money well spent because if the school system does not have this information, it is impossible for them to employ you. Therefore, the funds spent to seek employment should be considered an investment and not an expense. It is also advisable for you to send a photograph of yourself as you expect to present yourself for employment. Since time elapses between the campus interview and the in-system interview, recruiters sometimes forget faces and confuse person- nalities. A photograph could jog the memory of the prospective employer and thus increase your chances of being employed within a particular school system. Since most school systems must abide by recent civil rights legislation, they will not request a personal photograph. However, there are no laws which restrict you from voluntarily submitting a picture for their consideration.

SUMMARY. The above information outlines for you as a prospective beginning teacher just exactly what is expected of you in the process of seeking employment. There exist in different situations ramifications of the above process; however, in my opinion, the above process covers completely all the possibilities for applying for a teaching position. Individual school systems may differ to some degree, requiring more items or fewer. However, if you are prepared to submit the above items, you will be in an employable state with regard to every school system where you apply.

Although all of these items in one way or another involve a certain amount of expense for the prespective employee, they do make you more employable, thus once again it is my opinion that this expense is justifiable. It represents an investment in your future. After all you have invested nearly $10,000 and four years of your time to acquire a bachelor's degree in education. Now is the time to make the final investment and to begin reaping your justified returns.

CHAPTER II

WHERE TO APPLY

HOW TO JUDGE A SCHOOL SYSTEM. A prospective teacher in the area of elementary education wants some indication of the type of program in existence within the school system. Questions should be asked about the present reading program, language development program, social studies, science, and health programs. Questions should also be asked concerning the art, music, and physical education programs. Many teachers beginning their career find it undesirable to be saddled with the burden of teaching art, music, and physical education along with the normal academic subjects at the elementary level.

Questions should also be asked concerning the organizational arrangement of the various grade levels. For example, if the school system was arranged in a K 5-6 8-9 12 arrangement or a K 6-7 9-10 12 arrangement or a K 8-9 12 arrangement or a K 7-8 12 arrangement, this could affect the certification required by an applicant. A prospective teacher should also be interested in the flexibility allowed within time allocations set aside for each individual subject matter area. Areas of support within the school system must be considered. For example, benefits and services provided by speech therapist, economic education specialist, instrumental music instruction, librarian services, school psychologist, special education programs and classes and essential health services all contribute to a more desirable teaching situation. Pupil-teacher ratio is always an important aspect of every school system. For example, if a system has a pupil-teacher ratio exceeding the state recommendation, it can probably be concluded that funds are not available within the system to reduce this pupil-teacher ratio. Pupil-teacher ratio becomes increasingly important for a beginning teacher because, although studies do not prove statistically the advantage of teaching smaller groups, experience shows it is less difficult to individualize instruction with a smaller pupil-teacher ratio.

With regard to the middle school and secondary school program, the number of course offerings becomes an important element in the determination of the quality of programs. There should also be information available concerning the student goals, for example college-board students, technical, business, and nursing students immediate employment terminal students, and the number of students who enter the armed forces or get married immediately after graduation. Information concerning spending patterns within the school system are also important in determining the quality of the educational institution to which you are applying for employment. A general rule-of-thumb to follow in this area centers around the way money is spent. It is a long established fact that people spend money for what they consider important. Therefore, a school system spending pattern exposes completely its priorities with regard to program and teacher benefits.

WHAT QUESTIONS TO ASK. The following list of questions are for any interviewee to ask concerning the operation of a prospective school system:

1. Accreditation. By what institutions is the school system accredited?

2. Attendance. What is the average daily attendance within the school system?

3. Area of the school district. How many square miles encompass the school district?

4. Assessed evaluation. What is the present assessed evaluation within the school system and is there any hope for an increase in this evaluation in the near future?

5. Cafeteria service. What types of hot lunches are served in the school system and how much are pupils charged for these lunches?

6. School calendar. When does the school year begin, how many work days do teachers have during the year, and when is the ending day of the school year? (Also, questions could be asked in this area concerning spring breaks or spring recesses.)

7. Cost. What is the cost of instructing one pupil for one school year in the school system? What is the per hour cost of instruction within the system?

8. Graduates. What percentage of high school graduates enter college each year? What per cent are interested in some other form of advanced training? What is the drop-out rate each year? Is the system jointly affiliated with a vocational technical program?

9. Holidays. What holidays are teachers given each year as part of the school calendar?

10. Staff. How many certificated personnel are presently employed by the school system? How many of those people hold master's degrees? How many hold bachelor's degrees? How many non-degree teachers are presently employed by the school system? How many classified employees including custodians and bus drivers are employed by the school system presently?

11. Retirement. Is the school system affiliated with the state retirement system?

12. Salary schedule. What is the present beginning minimum salary for a bachelor's degree? What is the maximum salary for a bachelor's degree? What is the beginning minimum salary for a master's degree? How many actual principals and buildings are there within the system? Is a building principal assigned to each building within the system?

13. Tax rate in mills applied to the school system. How much millage is guaranteed from the tax dollars within the school system each year? Is there an anticipated increase in this millage in the near future and/or is there a need for an increase in this millage in the near future?

All of the questions are designed to allow a prospective candidate more information concerning a school system. Many recruiters will not have the answers to all of the questions during the preliminary interview. However, persistance in asking these questions at both the on-campus interview and in-system interview will gradually allow you to know more about the school system. If the recruiter seems ill at ease when asked these questions, simply move on to other subjects of conversation within the interview. Remember at all times that you have prepared for the interview with specific questions in mind. The interviewer is in the process of screening many people for different reasons; therefore, possibly the things that seem important to you as an interviewee will not seem equally important to him as an interviewer.

IS LOCATION IMPORTANT? When considering location in selecting a school system, it is important to keep in mind that location can be a limiting factor in your chances of obtaining employment, if it is construed to be too restrictive. It is most likely that you will want to locate in a school system similar to the one from which you graduated from high school. Teachers have long been categorized as "homers," meaning that their first preference in accepting a teaching position is usually in a school system of a comparable size to that from which they graduated. If you are in this classification, as long as the school system size meets with your approval, disregard geographic location as a limiting factor. In our society more and more professional people are becoming mobile. This mobility syndrome is not a result of accidental movement. It is necessitated by the changing demands of professional life. The best procedure to follow in considering location is an attitude of flexibility. If you are willing to locate where jobs become available, then your chances of finding a desirable position are increased manyfold.

HOUSING, RECREATION, AND SPECIAL INTEREST. A prospective teacher should inquire about the cost of housing in the area where he wishes to locate. Questions should also be asked concerning recreation in the area. If the individual has special interest in outdoor activities such as canoeing, skiing, boating and hiking, it would be to his advantage to inquire about availability of such activities before he accepts employment with a system. The cost of housing or of renting an apartment should be investigated thoroughly before accepting a contract with the school system. These inquires represent a common-sense approach to the logical problem of developing acceptable living conditions within the school district once you accept employment. If you are content with the living conditions, then you will also be more productive as a teacher. All these environmental influences contribute to your success as an educator and to the continued development of your reputation as a professional.

CHAPTER III

THE CONTRACT

LEGAL RIGHTS EVERY TEACHER SHOULD BE AWARE OF. Every teacher should realize that the Board of Education must notify him or her by April 30 of each year concerning his or her re-employment. If the Board desires not to re-employ a teacher, that Board of Education must notify the teacher of that fact before April 30. If the Board fails to do this, it is legally obligated to renew automatically that teacher's contract. A teacher, on the other hand, has until July 15 to accept or reject the Board's offer of a contract renewal. If a Board offers a teacher a contract on April 30 and the teacher does not respond to that offer by July 15, then the Board may at its discretion fill the position. Every beginning teacher should be aware of these two dates—April 30 (the Board must notify you) and July 15 (you must notify the Board).

WHEN TO SIGN A CONTRACT. When you as a teacher sign a contract, you are from that point forward obligated to the Board of Education. However, if you sign a contract and that contract is not acted upon by the Board of Education in a formal Board meeting, you have not yet been formally employed. Therefore, when recruiters or school officials offer you a contract and ask you to sign it, do not assume that just because you have signed a contract, you have been formally employed by the Board of Education. Your status as a formal employee of the school system does not commence until the Board of Education has acted upon the recommendation for your contract at a formal Board meeting. However, when seeking a position, it is tactful to sign a contract when it is offered to you regardless of whether or not you have authorization by the Board of Education. The reason for this is that by having you sign a contract the school official has at least informally obligated himself to employment for the coming school year. Although this obligation by a school official or administrator is not final until the Board acts upon it, you can feel assured that in most cases you have for all practical purposes been employed by that school system.

HOW TO GET A LEGAL RELEASE FROM A CONTRACT. From time to time you might find that you have signed a contract with a school system and in the meantime been offered a better salary or position with another school system. The question that then faces you is how to get a legal release from a signed contract. The first step is to request in writing to the school official who hired you a release from your present contract. It is a good policy to state the reason for your release in this letter. Although the Board of Education has no legal responsibility for granting a release at any given time, it is usually the Board policy to grant releases when teachers request them. The reason for this is obvious. It is better to grant a release from contract for a teacher than to have a dissatisfied teacher in the classroom. However, once again, remember that you are not legally released from a contract until the Board of Education has taken action on that release at a formal public Board meeting. Usually the new school system to which you are making application will require a copy of the Board minutes granting you a release from a previous contract. This copy of the Board minutes guarantees the new school official that you have been ethical throughout the process of selecting a new school system.

YOU AND BOARD OF EDUCATION POLICY. Although the above suggestions are generally true for most school systems, there are exceptions. Every school system has a formal set of Board of Education policies. It would be to your advantage as a beginning teacher to become thoroughly aware of these policies and even to study them in your leisure time. Board policies range from granting tenure and continuing contracts to rules and regulations governing discipline in the classroom and the responsibility of teachers in the hallways. To be thoroughly informed and to avoid any difficulties with the Board of Education, you should read especially the section of your Board of Education policy concerning resignations and the granting of contract release. In general, Board of Education policies are fair and in line with state law and procedures. However, occasionally you will find a

17

Board policy which is outdated or has not been revised for some time. If you find yourself in a position where you are in disagreement with a Board policy, the best procedure is to call this to the immediate attention of your supervisor, usually your principal.

HOW TO RESIGN. Although the process of resignation seems rather simple, it does have personal ramification. For example, if you do a poor job of resigning from a school system, there may be rumors lingering concerning whether you were asked to resign or whether you resigned of your own will. To avoid this situation, state your resignation in writing to the personnel manager in the school system or the superintendent, as soon as you know that you desire a release from your present contract. Be sure to include in this request all reasons surrounding your situation and explain why you desire the release. If possible, attend the Board meeting at which the Board of Education formally grants you a release from your present contractual responsibility. It is also helpful if you state some observations concerning the school system while you were employed there and indicate some of the benefits that you have received as a teacher as a result of working for that school system. All of these things make a resignation a pleasant experience rather than unpleasant, misunderstood one..

CHAPTER IV

YOU AND THE ADMINISTRATION AND BOARD OF EDUCATION

As a new professional in a school district, you should establish good rapport and working relationships with the Board of Education and the administration. The administration you are most likely to come in contact with would be your building principal and your instructional supervisor. When you were first interviewed, you were probably judged among other things on personal traits such as posture, grooming, poise, and voice. Character traits such as inititive and reliability were also considered. Most recruiters take into consideration learning traits such as knowledge of the subject matter, interest in the subject, and English usage. Now that you are hired, you will be judged according to new criteria.

Most school systems judge their teachers on the following basis:
1. Knowledge of subject matter
2. Teaching techniques
3. Ability in planning and organizing
4. Skill is questioning students and explaining answers
5. Judgment in the use of materials
6. Ability to secure pupil participation is class activities
7. Classroom atmosphere
8. Rapport with pupils, including discipline
9. General classroom control in student attitude

In one way or another these become the items which determine whether you are a good teacher or a poor teacher. They are usually judged on a three, four, or five-point scale, depending upon the system and the administration. At the end of periodic evaluation by the administration, you are usually counselled in a half-hour conference by your principal or supervisor. At the end of the conference, it is indicated to you whether your contract will be renewed for the coming year or whether you will be placed on some kind of a conditional contract for a trial teaching period to

19

determine whether or not you have the ability to overcome your difficulties.

ORGANIZATION AND PLANNING. The quickest and most successful route to good teaching is, in my opinion, complete planning and organization of lessons. Let planning and organization be your guide to your first successful experience in education. Plan your daily lessons and have your plans available for administrators to review. Follow your lesson plans and don't be afraid to revise and evaluate your planning and organizational procedure after each class session. Involve students and parents in your planning activities. Arrange each lesson plan for a purpose and state your purpose in terms of behavioral objectives of changes in children's behavior. Never forget to explain to your students what they have learned as well as the subject matter. Try to summarize all of your lessons each day, thus giving your students something to carry home with them to their parents when they ask the question, "What did you learn today?"

COOPERATION. Cooperation is a key word for the beginning teacher. Look at your first experience in education as a learning experience as well as a professional experience. Cooperate with all administrators and key personnel throughout the school system in planning and organizing your lessons. Cooperate with fellow staff members and students in the organization and development of the school social atmosphere. In general, be cooperative and helpful to your fellow staff members as well as your superiors. Try always to follow the rules of the school system and when in doubt, consult an administrator for direction.

DISCIPLINE. Discipline is another key word in the school business. Many studies carried out by professional organizations have indicated that taxpayers are more concerned with discipline than any other part of the school program. As a teacher you have a direct responsibility for maintaining discipline within the classroom, but do not restrict yourself to discipline in the classroom. expand your area of operation to include hallways, gymnasiums, and student activities within the building. Never develop the habit of turning your head the other way when you see some activity taking place that needs the strong hand and attention of a disciplinarian. Pride yourself in being able to control student behavior and whenever possible maintain your own discipline without help from others. The everyday discipline of students in the classroom is a difficult and challenging responsibility all beginning teachers must face. Accept this responsibility and do your best to become known as a good disciplinarian.

EVALUATION OF STUDENTS. "Firm but fair," "friendly but not familar" are good phrases to describe a teacher's role in carrying out good evaluation and discipline procedures. Here again, organization is the answer. Develop an accurate set of records of students' behavior in the classroom. Always discuss an individual student's problems with him first. When evaluating student progress, remember that you must have a complete record of student performance in order to make an accurate evaluation. Most educators admit that no matter how you evaluate students, in the last analysis it remains a subjective judgment. However, a subjective evaluation that is not based upon some kind of record keeping procedure can be criticized. To protect yourself against criticism in the evaluation of students, use some method of recording grades. Assign classroom work as well as homework regularly and give a series of quizzes or examinations throughout any given grading period. Record the grades of all this work either in percentages, in numerical values, or in letter grades and average the results of your record keeping each six-or nine-week period. Be fair with students, in general, and give them the benefit of a doubt. Remember, if a student fails in your class, you have failed also to some extent as a teacher. Keeping this golden rule in mind, try to evaluate students in a fair and consistent manner. Pride yourself in being a fair evaluator. It is better to give a student the benefit of a doubt and be wrong than it is to criticize him harshly on unfounded evaluative procedures.

ACCEPTING EVALUATION YOURSELF. No one likes to be criticized, especially professional educators who have spent four years in a university learning how to teach. However, any evaluation that is made of your performance is subjective, as is any evaluation that you make of a student's performance. If you receive a critical evaluation, try to accept it as constructive criticism. Try

21

to do everything possible to please your evaluator. If after a period of time you repeatedly receive unsuccessful evaluation, it might be necessary for you to ask your principal or evaluator to arrange to have you evaluated by some other member of the staff. It does no good whatsoever to argue with an evaluator. If the person evaluating you feels strongly enough about your behavior to criticize it, then no argument in the world is likely to change his opinion. The best procedure to follow is avoidance or correction. If, in your opinion, it is impossible to correct the situation, then try to avoid it. A permanent negative evaluation in your personnel file could jeopardize your chances of ever regaining employment as a teacher. At all cost protect your reputation as a professional educator. Once you have received repeated negative evaluations and they have been filed in your personal folder, your chance to succeed as a teacher is much diminished. Although no one expects you to accept criticism openly and with a smile, try to develop a graciousness and poise in accepting others' subjective judgment of your behavior. This approach shows both confidence and maturity and in the long run will speak for itself to both your peers and your superiors.

CHAPTER V

YOU AND TEACHER ORGANIZATIONS

Today more than ever teacher organizations are becoming increasingly unionized. This union activity and the ensuing reputations developed by teacher organizations have a direct effect upon you and your chances of being employed by a school system. Most recruiters screen applicants with regard to militant attitudes towards established organizational procedures and political attitudes toward active participation in union-like activities. It is a little accepted but very real fact that this becomes part of the screening procedure when employing teachers within a school system. During the last few years, I have frequently discussed this matter with my colleagues and have found to my amazement how much credence is paid to this as a negative criterion in selecting teachers for a school system.

JOINING TEACHER ORGANIZATIONS. Many school systems throughout the United States have compulsory memberships in teacher organizations. These organizations range from local education associations to local unionized associations. Most of the organizations require both membership in the local organization and the parent organization at the state level, leaving membership in the national organization as an option of the individual teacher. Fees and organizational dues constitute a large deduction from a beginning teacher's income. However, many school systems today are organized very much like what used to be called a closed shop. "Closed shop" policy here means that organization membership is compulsory within the school district. Although there are school systems of this type in operation in the U. S., many systems, and especially smaller ones, do not require organizational membership. Of course, in the last analysis, whether or not you join a professional organization is a decision that you alone can make. My advice is that if you actively and strongly support education association membership or unionized education association activities, it would be to your advantage in applying for a position not to express your feelings with regard to the activities of these organizations. The reason is very obvious. Many administrators in personnel management positions today have been irritated for one reason or another by unionized activities as a result of their association with teachers' organizations. For this reason they tend to view critically positive and active support of some of the functions of these organizations. Some of this resentment toward organizations is due to the negotiation process in which Boards of Education actively negotiate such items as teachers' salaries with members from the teacher organitions. These sessions are usually lengthy and heated discussions of the rights and responsibilities of the Board of Education and the teachers' organization. For this reason if you support a teachers' organization and its functions strongly, it would be to your advantage not to make aggressive support obvious to an interviewer.

SUPPORTING A TEACHERS' ORGANIZATION. During the process of selection some school systems will directly ask a candidate whether or not he will strike against the Board of Education. This is a difficult question to answer. It has been my experience that most prospective teachers answer this question negatively. They say that they would not strike against the school system no matter what the circumstances. However, little do they realize that when the question is asked, they cannot anticipate the pressures that might be placed upon them to conform to strike activities. For example, would you as a prospective teacher strike if all the other teachers in the building struck? No matter what your philosophical position is with regard to teacher organizations, you as a prospective teacher must be prepared to face the issues and take a position with regard to how much or how little you will support a local teachers' organization or union.

HOLDING OFFICE IN A TEACHERS' ORGANIZATION. In most cases as a new teacher in a school system you will not be asked to assume an office in a teachers' organization. These positions are usually reserved for experienced teachers within the system. However, it is my advice that the first year or two that you teach, you should observe very carefully the activities and functions of the officers of the organization. And then on the basis of your experience and knowledge about the philosophy and functions of the organization, you must personally decide whether you want to avail yourself of the possible animosity generated by playing such a role within the school system. Your primary function is that of teaching, not of politics. In many school systems today an over-concentration on the political side of the organization and lack of concentration on the academic responsibilities of a teacher some-times mean disaster in terms of professional image within the school system.

PARTICIPATION IN ORGANIZATION SPONSORED ACTIVITIES WITHIN THE SCHOOL SYSTEM. As a new teacher in a school system, you must participate in all functions sponsored by the local education association. Your participation is mandatory for obvious reasons. These people are your colleagues and will work with you on a daily basis. Therefore, their friendship and support are invaluable to you. For this reason you must actively belong to a teachers' organization and participate in activities it sponsors. However, participation does not mean outward resistance toward the establishment in the form of the Board of Education. There is a distinct difference between participating in social functions sponsored by the education association and outwardly demonstrating against the policies set forth by the Board of Education. You as a beginning teacher must weigh these responsibilities carefully and in accordance with your political power and personal ambition to survive and continue teaching within the school system. Although stated very practically, these questions are deeply in-volved in personal philosophy of and approach to education. The advice given is purely for the purpose of gaining employment within a system and maintaining your professional image as an educator.

CHAPTER VI

YOU AND THE COMMUNITY

As a new teacher in a new community, you should realize that you have certain responsibilities to yourself and to your profession. Your reputation as a teacher and as a professional educator depend completely upon the image that you create as you work and live in the community that surrounds you. All professional educators realize the political aspect of maintaining a professional image within the community. However, the final decision as to whether or not you want to isolate yourself from the community or participate in its functions is a decision that you personally must make.

WHAT IS DEMANDED. As a first-year professional in the community, it is accurate to say that not much is demanded of you from a personal standpoint. As long as your activities are morally and ethically acceptable and your behavior in the classroom is professional and responsible, the first year of your teaching experience will be pretty much politically uneventful. If after the first year you continue to teach in a community, other factors may be taken into consideration, depending on its size. For example, if you are living in a small community, you will be expected to participate in church and social functions. In a larger community you can become more easily uninvolved with community activities. As you circulate throughout the community, it is expected that you will be well groomed; that you will act in a responsible manner with regard to yourself and your friends; that you will not participate in any illegal activities or immoral functions. I have, for example, known teachers to lose their jobs because of their failure to groom themselves properly when appearing in public, or because certain Board of Education members felt that their personal friends were undersirable. These are facts of life in professional education and although many of us might disagree with the purpose and foundation of these facts, we still must live with them.

WHAT IS EXPECTED. In most communities regardless of size, it is expected that a new member of the community will take an active part in church and social functions. Most communities want to believe that members of the teaching profession represent stability and, therefore, should be active in such civic groups as scouting, YMCA, and other social organizations. Holding office in community organizations is also an asset in developing your professional image within the community. Studying and learning the power structure in the community and operating within its confines are considered necessary for guaranteeing employment with the local school system over a prolonged period of time. Good relationships and rapport with your colleagues and administrators throughout the school system are expected of you as a new teacher. In many communities it is assumed that you will get married and raise a family, becoming a permanent part of the community. Although these items are in no way written into your contract as a beginning teacher, on a practical level most communities in the United States expect educators to act and be something special within the society. Therefore, in thinking of long-term success in a community, one should consider all the factors that have been reviewed. This does not mean that ignoring one or more of the above factors will necessarily guarantee failure, but rather that by following the above course of action your success in the community and in the teaching profession and the development of your professional image is more likely to be successful.

WHAT IS OPTIONAL. Complete and immediate adaptation to the local political and religious biases is, of course, neither expected nor required. Take your time, learn the situation in which you are working and understand it for what it is. Take a practical analytical approach, then make a decision as to whether this is the kind of situation with which you are willing to work and grow. If it is not, then you will have to think in terms of a transfer to another school system. However, if you feel that you can exist within this situation and survive according to the political, religious, and social ideals expected of a teacher in a community such as the one in which you find yourself, then you have found a professional home and can begin to develop your image within the community. All behavior is optional in that you must make the decision as to how much of your personality you are willing to adjust or change in order to conform to the expectations of the community which employs you. Remember that the community views you as a model which they expect their children to follow. If you, as a beginning teacher, do not meet with the community's approval for one reason or another, then over a period of time, the school system will probably not renew your contract or will ask you to resign your position. You can gather evidence as to how a community reacts to an undesirable by observing your fellow teachers and how they are accepted or rejected by the community which they serve. You will find after a very short time that it is obvious when a teacher is undesirable to the community in which he works. You will start hearing hypercritical remarks from locals in the community which are directed at his professional ability and expertise. All of these hints and comments become your guide as to what is and is not acceptable within the community where you work. Be observant and be logical in your approach to the conditions in which you must work. If they are desirable and you find no personal limitations inhibiting your acceptance of these foundational philosophies, then you have found a home here in the education profession. If you find that you are truly averse to some of the expectations of the community, then your alternatives are clear cut: you must resign your position and look elsewhere or meet resistance within the community you serve.

CHAPTER VII

ADVANCEMENT AND TRANSFERS

Like all teachers before you, sooner or later you will have to decide what you expect for yourself in the field of education. As you consider the various alternatives to satisfy your ambitions, it is almost certain that advancement within the system will become one possibility. Although it seems it should be a uncomplicated process to advance from an elementary teaching position to that of an elementary principal or from secondary teaching to secondary principal, in actuality, it is not so. Another factor which will face you as a second- or third-year teacher will be that of transfers. If you are dissatisfied with the administrator under whom you are working, you might feel that a transfer to another building within the system is the answer to your problem. Both advancements and transfers have their idiosyncrasies with regard to accomplishing them within any given educational system. In fact, your entire performance as a teacher comes to the fore when you request a transfer or an advancement. No matter how well you do your job and carry out your responsibilities as a classroom teacher, there will be certain people throughout the community and within the school system who are for one reason or another dissatisfied with you and your performance. For example it might be a parent who feels that you unjustly evaluated his or her child; an administrator who feels your activity within the school system does not meet his approval; or it might be various conservative segments of the community who disapprove of a liberal class in socialism you taught in which you explained the merits of communism. Whatever the situation, always remember that no matter how well you carry out your responsibilities, it is always possible that someone is dissatisfied with you. As a result, if you plan to advance within a system or you plan to transfer from one building to another, it is important that you began to lay groundwork far in advance of your actually achieving it.

ADVANCEMENT AND TRANSFERS WITHIN THE SYSTEM. Transfers within the system are for the most part easier to achieve than transfers to another school system. However, it must be kept in mind that any request for a transfer should be far in advance of the time that you actually want it to take place. You should also remember that when requesting a transfer from your immediate supervisor, you should assure him that you will be more than happy to continue in your present capacity if the desired transfer is not available at the time you make the request. In other words, humility and cooperation in asking for a change in position within the system is a good basic attitude to take. If you are aggressive and ask for the change for a negative reason—for example, inability to communicate with an administrator or a parent in the present situation—this can be construed as a general weakness in your ability to perform your responsibility. Also it is not good to ask for a transfer each year. This shows a weakness on your part to adapt to new situations and to be satisfied with a situation permanently. For example, if you ask for a transfer for the next school year and receive it, you should expect to maintain your new position for at least two or three years before asking for another transfer within the system. These are basic ground rules for dealing with the administrative powers that influence you. There can be exceptions in each situation. However, in general, I feel that these ground rules represent a logical approach to the problem of achieving a transfer within a school system.

ADVANCEMENT OR TRANSFER INTO ANOTHER SCHOOL SYSTEM. An advancement or transfer into another school system is always a serious business. It involves moving your professional reputation and credentials from one school system and community to another. This move must successfully transplant you and your position in the new system. For this reason there are many factors which should be considered when transferring from one school system to another. No matter what kind of impression you make upon the person who interviews you for the new position, you must always remember that you are carrying your old reputation with you in terms of your recommendations. You should therefore select proper people to provide recommendations for you when you are transferring to another system. Your immediate supervisor and his recommendations are always most valuable in seeking a new position. If your immediate supervisor will not give you a good recommendation or if you have doubts about the kind of recommendation that he will give you, it is better to avoid a recommendation from him than to get a poor one. If you are faced with this situation and cannot get a good recommendation from your immediate supervisor, then possibly your best route would be to ask his supervisor for a recommendation if he knows of your work and activity within the system. It is always good to have two or more recommendations from your previous employment; however, be very careful to select people that you feel confident will give you good recommendations. A poor recommendation in your credentials could cost you a future job. If it is completely impossible for you to find good reference within the system, then you will have to look outside the system to your friends and acquaintances in the community where you work. Although these references are not as good as references within the system, they are better than poor references from your immediate supervisor. Whenever you leave a system, there is always doubt as to whether you are leaving on a voluntary basis or whether you are being forced out of the system for some reason. The best way to set aside all rumors with regard to why you are leaving is to explain fully to your friends and your supervisor what you plan to do in the future as a result of your leaving the system. Therefore, it is better to have a position in mind when you hand in your resignation than it is to hand in an unexplained resignation which will have much doubt and suspicion attached to it. You should be able to explain exactly what you have in mind for your professional future.

When you move from one system to another, you must take with you your complete up-to-date sick leave records and the number of years' experience teaching in the system along with recommendations from your supervisor or your immediate administrative contact. It should also be noted that experience can be a disadvantage in moving from one system to another as well as an advantage. For example, most school systems hire young, inexperiences teachers because they cost the school system less money. A first-year teacher begins at the bottom of the salary schedule where a teacher with three or four or five years' experience begins teaching higher on the salary schedule. There have been no studies which prove that experience improves teaching. All school systems are well aware of teachers who have several years' experience and are still doing poor jobs in the classroom. For this reason a large number of years of experience can be a detriment to your changing a position. If you truly want a new position in a system, it might be to your advantage upon certain occasions to ask to come to the school system on the salary schedule with less experience than you have actually had. This can be accomplished in several ways. The most common is to simply indicate that you have had fewer years' experience than you have actually had in the profession.

Occasionally it is necessary for a teacher to leave a system because he is asked to resign. If this is your case, then the best route for you to follow before regaining your employment is to go back to the university and take additional work. Additional courses in the university legitimize your reason for leaving the school system. Upon completing your work at the university, you then are ready to attempt to regain employment with another school system. The time you spent in the university between the time you are asked to resign from the school system and the time you attempt to regain employment re-establishes you as a professional educator. Most recruiters will not ask why you left the previous school system if you simply indicate you left to return to school for additional education. Therefore, it makes it much easier for you to regain employment from the university and from the academic setting than it would if you attempted to regain employment in another school system after you had been terminated. Hopefully you will not be involved in a situation like this. However, all of us have weak years and it is possible that you too could be involved in a resignation or forced termination.

Remember that when you leave a school system, you are finished with that school system. It is better to leave a good impression behind than it is to complain about something you disliked in the system. You are a professional and you are supposed to overlook some of the human weaknesses of others.

CHAPTER VIII

INVESTING WHAT YOU EARN AS A TEACHER

With the coming of higher salary schedules in education, you must have an idea about how to manage the money that you earn, especially since in the field today it is important that you continue your own education after completion of your bachelor's degree. Education has become a costly process, and saving and investing your earnings can help you finance the future education you need to continue to be successful in your profession. Because of budgetary cutbacks in school systems and common financial trouble among public school systems today, you should protect yourself against future financial developments that may affect you as a teacher. For example, if a school system cuts back its program, you as a beginning teacher are low in terms of seniority and therefore stand to lose your teaching position. You should save and invest some of the money you earn in order that you might be able to exist financially until you find another position. The following are a few helpful hints to investing which, it is hoped, will help you handle your money successfully:

ANNUITIES. Annuities are a common type of investment available from most insurance agents and some school systems. As a teacher in the United States you are eligible to participate in tax sheltered annuities. This simply means you are eligible to deduct a certain portion of your income each month to be paid into an insurance type policy which allows you to earn money on your investment and, upon retirement, draw back the money you have invested as a savings. In general tax sheltered annuities are good. However, be careful to deal with a reputable insurance agency and be sure you are financially able to deduct or save the amount of money suggested by the agent. The advantage is that you do not have to pay income taxes on the amount deducted from your pay check to participate in an annuity program. This allows your income tax to be less each year and as a result allows you a financial advantage over non-teaching professions.

RETIREMENT SYSTEMS. Today every state in the United States has some type of a teachers' retirement system. These range from social security to private systems developed and operated by the state. All retirement systems are a type of savings and should be looked upon favorably. In most systems there are provisions which allow you, upon leaving the profession, to withdraw all the funds that you have paid into the retirement system. It would be to your advantage to study the retirement system which is offered by your Board of Education. In general, I would say as a beginning teacher you would want to participate in a retirement system. Although retirement is a long way off, many of these systems have fringe benefits. For example, if you become ill after five years' service, some systems will pay your retirement for the rest of your life just as if you had worked thirty years in the profession. Usually the Board of Education matches the amount of money you pay into the retirement system; therefore, your funds multiply and grow. If you have an opportunity to participate in a retirement system when you take your first teaching position, it would be my suggestion that you study this alternative very carefully and choose to participate.

CREDIT UNION. Credit unions represent a sharing of available money. All school systems do not have credit unions, but, today credit unions are a common type of financial organization. Usually a certain amount of money which you determine will be deducted from your pay check each month. These funds accumulate in what is called a credit union. Usually credit unions are organized and the officers are teachers within the school system. You can borrow money from a credit union for a reduced rate of interest. Credit unions in general have more advantages than disadvantages. Usually they pay high rates of interest and allow you to borrow money at a lower rate than do banks and loan companies. Whether or not you participate in a credit union is, of course, your choice. However, as a new teacher in a community, a credit union could in many cases aid you in maintaining your financial stability.

BANKS AND LOAN COMPANIES. Everyone is familiar with the national banks and savings and loan companies. However, many savings and loan companies pay higher rates of interest than do

34

national banks. Therefore, if you are starting a savings account in a community, it might be to your advantage to check out the interest rates on passbook accounts. Usually you will find that savings and loan companies pay the highest passbook savings rate. Although this amounts to very little in terms of a total year's earnings, it does help in financing your livelihood as a new member in the educational profession.

INCOME TAX ADVANTAGES. There are many good books available on the advantages of being a teacher with regard to your income tax. As a beginning teacher it is possible that this is the first time in your life that you have had earnings in the amount of your first year's wages. For this reason you should understand the income tax advantages open to you as a member of the teaching profession. For example, as a teacher you may deduct the depreciation on your professional library, the cost of maintaining an office in your apartment or home, transportation you provide yourself in carrying out your teaching responsibilities for which you are not reimbursed by the Board of Education, time, energy, and materials you expend in extracurricular activities sponsored by the school system. These are just a few of the tax deductions open to you as a teacher. By carefully checking the tax laws you might find that you can deduct a vacation to Europe during the summer when you improve your skill in French or some other language. You might also find that you can deduct the cost of your additional education as a member of the profession, including tuition, books, room and meals when you are forced to study in some other location. When it comes time for you to move to another school system or to transfer to another position, your moving expenses are a deductable item on your income tax. Although some of these items are commonly deductable for everyone, your professional library and an office in your home are items which are of special significance to teachers. Remember as a member of the new profession, it is your responsibility to protect yourself and to learn about the advantages of being a teacher.

CHAPTER IX

MISCELLANEOUS FACTORS

DATA SHEET. Your personal data sheet or vitae is an important part of finding a job as a new teacher. In Appendix A you will see an example of a completed data sheet, which you might use as a guide in making out your own personal data sheet. Enclose a personal data sheet with each letter of application you send to a prospective school system. Remember your data sheet represents you, so be careful of spelling and grammar and about the contents of the data sheet.

POLITICAL APPOINTMENTS IN EDUCATION. With competition in education so active today, the problem of political appointments becomes increasingly prevalent. In many school systems it is possible to gain a position through a political appointment, for example, if you know personally a member of the Board of Education, or you have friends who work for the school system. However, as a general rule, I would not suggest dependence upon political appointments as a means of gaining a teaching position. Many recruiters frown upon attempts to use pressure through personal contacts to achieve a position within a system. In fact in some systems just the fact that you mention a member of the Board of Education or another teacher in the system as a reference might disallow you a position depending upon the individual recruiter's attitude toward political contacts. Study the situation in which you are applying very carefully before attempting to use political pressure to gain a teaching position. Some people are hired in this way, but in general people are hired on the basis of their achievement, personal background, and personality. A political appointment guarantees you nothing but immediate employment within the system. Once your political contact becomes unseated or his position changes within the community, you may find yourself at the mercy of the person you pressured into hiring you. As a beginning teacher, be extremely careful about using your connections within a community to gain a position within the school system.

COMPETITION FOR POSITIONS. Competition for teaching positions today is at an all-time high. As a result, certain teaching fields are more difficult to enter than others. For example, a recent study completed by the National Education Association shows that the greatest need for teachers is in vocational-technical fields. The least demand for teachers is in the area of social studies. This year more than ever there is an increased supply of teachers in the area of language arts and social studies. If you are a teacher in one of these disciplines, you can count on more competition in getting a position than teachers in the vocational-technical areas. However, you should keep in mind that the supply and demand for educators usually runs on about a four-year cycle. For example, four years from now, due to population growth and the fact that teachers are being discouraged from entering the field of education, the supply and demand will equalize. It would be my advice that if a teacher graduating from college this year with a bachelor's degree cannot find a position, the best investment that he could make in his future would be to complete his master's degree. By the time he completes his master's degree (within two or three years) there should be a position awaiting him and the demand should have been raised to a point which would justify his prolonging his entrance into the field for the additional years needed to obtain an advanced degree.

Being aware of the competition present for teaching positions can be your greatest asset in achieving employment. Time and time again prospective candidates enter my office with the idea that the school system is doing them a favor by interviewing them. This kind of an attitude can only yield negative results. Understanding that you are in competition for a position can give you a fine edge in terms of your attitude toward employment. Prepare yourself psychologically for the screening process and groom yourself to provide the proper responses to the inquires which confront you. Competition is good for the teaching profession. In the long run it eliminates incompetent, poor, and uninterested teachers, thus making the task of education easier for all of those dedicated professionals who remain in positions of responsibility.

SCREENING PROCEDURE. When applying for a teaching position, there are many factors you should take into consideration. Different recruiters and personnel men use different screening procedures to eliminate candidates. Some rely completely on tangible evidence such as credentials, transcripts, and application forms. If a candidate fails to provide one of these three items, he is automatically eliminated from consideration for a position. Although this process seems harsh, keep in mind that most recruiters have from ten to fifty applicants for every position they have open within the system. Therefore, to many, any screening procedure which eliminates people is satisfactory. Those applicants surviving after the initial screening are then screened by the personnel manager himself. Keep in mind that not only his opinion of you is important in the screening process; other factors are as well. For example, as you enter the office for your initial interview, be careful how you approach other individuals in the office. Secretaries, bookkeepers, and other administrators within the office, by chatting with you, might have a different impression of your personality than you give the recruiter. Perhaps you have developed an appearance you wish to make in the interview. However, if you have your mask off between the time you enter the building for the interview and the time the interview actually takes place, it is possible that someone might observe some negative quality in your personality and pass this on to the interviewer, thus eliminating you as a candidate for a position. Once again credentials become an important part of the screening procedure. It has been my experience that time and time again applicants provide me with a poor set of credentials. Of course, when they request the university to send their credentials to my office, they have no idea that they may have negative recommendations included in their professional credentials. Although there is no way to insure completely against having a person you think would support your talents provide you with a negative recommendation, there are ways to detect negative recommendations within your credentials. Once you surmise that you have been interviewed for several positions without being successful, you might contact your placement director and have him personally review your credentials to see if you have a negative recommendation among them. Although your placement director in most cases will not tell you the name of the individual who has given you the negative recommendation, he will upon your request remove recommendations, while preserving the confidential nature of placement office's responsibility toward the applicant and the employer.

In any event, everything you say and do, including the way that you appear, has an impact upon whether you are employed by a recruiter. For that reason it is extremely important that you take great care to develop the kind of image that you wish to perpetuate within the interview.

RESEARCHING THE SYSTEM. There are many and diversified questions one might ask when researching the system. For example:

1. How many teachers are employed by the system?
2. How many students are enrolled in the system?
3. What is the pupil-teacher ratio of the system?
4. How many buildings are there in the system?
5. Does each building have full-time administrator?
6. How many elective courses are there at the secondary level?
7. What kind of scheduling is there at the secondary level?
8. Is there a tri-basal individualized reading program in the elementary schools?
9. Are there special teachers for the elementary schools in the area of art, music, and physical education?
10. Are beginning teachers allowed to experiment with innovative programs within the system?
11. How is the curriculum developed and what kind of organizational chart is there for curriculum decision making?
12. How rigidly does the system adhere to the line-of-command concept of school administration?
13. How many text books are presently being used in the system that are beyond five years of age?
14. How is a beginning teacher expected to behave with regard to teachers' organizations?
15. Is membership in teachers' organizations mandatory within the system?

16. Is there a negotiated salary schedule within the system?
17. What is the salary for beginning teachers with a bachelor's degree?
18. What fringe benefits are available within the school system?
19. Are teachers allowed to attend professional conferences and does the Board pay for these?
20. Does the system have special services of psychologists, speech and hearing therapists, and learning disabilities consultants at all grade levels?
21. Are there special education classes for educably mentally retarded and neurologically handicaped students?
22. What are the expectations of a beginning teacher within the system?

Although there are many other questions which a beginning teacher may ask an interviewer, the above questions generally give you a complete picture of a school system and its operation. Any other questions in which you are particularily interested you should develop in your own mind during the interview. It is not good taste, however, to bring the list with you in the actual interview. It is much better to ask these questions informally and in a relaxed way as they fit into the normal flow of conversation between yourself and the interviewer.

PERSONAL ATTITUDE TOWARD THE INTERVIEW. Your personal attitude toward interviewing is a primary factor in determining whether or not you will be hired by a school system. You must personally determine what your goal is with regard to the interview. Are you just investigating the school system to find out what kind of a system it is or are you seriously interested in gaining employment? If you are interested in gaining employment, all of your questions and responses should be directed toward that end. Do not digress into other areas. Stick to the subject of employment, ask questions directly, accept answers graciously and do not put the interviewer on the spot. For example, if you ask the interviewer a question and he hesitates, move very quickly to another question. You are the only person who can psychologically analyze what is expected by the interviewer. This is your first goal. Listen carefully and observe the interviewer, his remarks and opinions. Whenever possible withhold your ideas until the interviewer has committed himself. Your ability as an interviewee to analyze the interviewer and project the desired responses to his inquires can be your key to success in the interview situation. Try to maintain a cool, calm, and collected attitude toward the process of interviewing. Be relaxed, prepared, and confident that you can do the job and accept the responsibility expected of you within the school system. Always keep foremost in your mind that you have nothing to lose because when you came to the interview, you did not have the job; therefore, anything you do that is positive during the interview can bring you closer to gaining your goal of employment. If you leave the office unsuccessful, the only thing that you have lost has been the opportunity. You have gained valuable experience in the interviewing process which can help you become more successful during your next interview. Be conscious of and honest about your mistakes during the interview. After the interview is completed evaluate your own performance and try to analyze the purpose of the questions asked during the interview. This technique will enable you to become more familiar with the process by which selection is made and will help you to be successful in future interviews.

HOME TOWN TEACHING. As mentioned earlier, teachers have long been considered a group of "homers." This statement simply means that most teachers after graduating from college desire to teach in a school system similar to the one from which they graduated in high school. It can also refer to the prospective teacher's desire to return to a home town situation. There are distinct advantages in teaching in one's home town. For example, housing may not be a problem since an unmarried teacher might live at home with parents or relatives. A beginning teacher understands the value system of his home town and therefore has fewer adjustment difficulties with regard to what is expected of him or her. Since most of us have many social and political contacts within our own home community, these factors also become advantages to teaching in one's home town. Relatives and friends become supportive elements of a teacher's profession in the home town

41

situation. This also is an important factor in determining the success or failure of the first professional attempt in a new teacher's life. Familiarity with the school system from which the teacher graduated also contributes to his or her ability to adapt to the system and function in accordance with administrative desires. Although it is obvious that there are many advantages to returning to a home town teaching situation the disadvantages should also be considered.

Some of the disadvantages include overfamiliarity with people in the community. For example, you as a beginning teacher starting the teaching profession on the high school level might find yourself on a first-name basis with many of the students. Since you are already known in the community, it is possible that many people have opinions about your abilities. These opinions can be negative as well as positive and can contribute to your failure as well as your success. Returning to your home community you might also find that many of your old teachers are still in the system and they possibily could have negative opinions about your ability and/or apptitude for the teaching profession. Since you attended school in the community, the likelihood is that you will have to prove yourself as a professional. It may be more difficult for you to be accepted into the professional cliques within the community and within the professional organization of the area. In general, if you return to a home community, you are a "known quanity." This means that the community has already developed opinions and expectations about you and your ability. All of these factors, plus the political aspects of returning to one's home community, can contribute negatively to the possibility of your success as a teacher. Although in the final analysis this is a decision which only you can make, be sure you take into consideration the disadvantages of teaching in your home community.

SOME TIPS ON HOW YOUR INQUIRIES ARE PROGRESSING. After you have made several inquiries into prospective teaching positions, you are bound to be curious about how these inquiries are progressing. There are several ways that you can tell whether or not you are being seriously considered for a teaching position. Have you been contacted by telephone by the school system? It is more expensive to telephone than it is to write a prospective candidate. Many school systems only use the telephone when they are seriously considering a candidate for appointment. Did the school system invite you to telephone them at their expense? This is usually another indication of serious consideration of you. Did the school system pay your expenses to the interview? If so, this is an indication that they are seriously considering hiring you. Did the school system contact you first or did you contact the school system first? If they contacted you first, of course, this is an indication of their interest in your teaching for them. Did the personnel director give you a definite time indication as to when you would be contacted again by the school system? If he did not, you can assume that you are not seriously being considered for an immediate position. Did he discuss exact grade levels with you? If he did, there is a good chance that he has a position in mind for which he is considering your appointment. Of course, the positive or negative tone of the interview always provides some indication of seriousness on the part of both the applicant and the employer. The tone of the interview, therefore, should be considered when trying to analyze how seriously you are being considered for a teaching position. The frequency of contact between you and the school system is another good indication of whether or not the system wants you. All of these factors go together in determining whether or not you'll be employed by a school system. Be very sensitive to the reaction of the school system to your inquiries; otherwise you will have no indication of where you stand with regard to employment.

HOW DO RECRUITERS CHOOSE CANDIDATES? There exist many criteria upon which prospective candidates are chosen for employment within a given school system. Some of these are as follows:
1. Girls' physical education teachers should have a feminine image.
2. Male elementary teachers should have a masculine image.
3. One should always look at prospective music teachers carefully because many of the men have feminine tendencies.
4. Football coaches and other athletic coaches should be teachers first and coaches second.

5. Dirty fingernails and dandruff in one's hair are good indications of shoddy grooming and shoddy preparation for the classroom.

6. Confident teachers have fewer discipline problems than do insecure teachers.

7. A strong voice controls a classroom better than a soft voice.

8. Typed applications show initative and reliability.

9. Handwriting is in general a good indication of neatness and order within the personality.

10. Misspelled words on the application show lack of concern for detail and in turn lack of concern for detailed knowledge of subject matter.

11. Overinterest in salary indicates lack of concern for subject matter and teaching in general.

12. Overconcern for social and political activism within the community is an indicator for teacher troublemakers.

13. Correct English usage is a good indication of academic ability.

14. Good posture and good grooming contribute to a healthy image in the classroom.

Although these items represent only a few considerations by recruiters, they do indicate how subjectively each candidate is evaluated. Although documentation is not available in support of these contentions, it is my firm belief that many recruiters consider them heavily in appointing prospective teachers.

CERTIFICATION IN TEACHING AND RECIPROCITY BETWEEN STATES. Each state now has a division of state teacher certification. An agreement has been reached between most states in the United States granting reciprocity with one another. This means that if you hold a teaching certificate in one state and apply for a teaching certificate in another state, you will be granted a reciprocal certificate equivalent to the one that you are holding within the first state. For example, in Ohio there are provisional certificates, professional certificates and permanent certificates. There are also certificates for administrators and special education personnel. In other states, such as Michigan, they have no administrative certificates. Still other states have more divisions of

certification than do Ohio. You should seriously check into the
certification requirements within the state of your choice. Become
familiar with the various grades of certificates and the qualification
needed to advance from one certificate to another. Although this
is not important in your first one or two years of teaching, it
becomes increasingly important as you accumulate years of experience and look forward to retirement from the teaching profession.
In many states your job security depends to some extent upon the
certification that you possess. If you are considering a move from
one state to another, you should always first consider whether you
are certified in the new state of your choice. In order to determine
your certification status within any given state, write the Depart-
ment of Education, in care of the Capitol Building of that state,
send along a copy of your present certification and ask what your
status would be with regard to certification within that state. All
of these things take a little of your time and some postage, but
they are well worthwhile in aiding you with a smooth transition
from one state to another. Your professional status depends upon
your certification within a given state. By moving from one state
to another, it is possible that you would lose your active status
in some aspects of school business. Your ultimate goal is to reach
a status of permanent or life certification within any state. This
will normally make you eligible for tenure or continuing contract
within a local school system. This status of tenure or continuing
contract is a permanent status which will allow you job security
in the teaching profession.

LIMITED AND CONTINUING CONTRACTS. Limited contract
means that the school system is obligated to you on a limited
basis. Most limited contracts run for one year. However, in some
cases two- and three-year limited contracts are issued. Continuing
contracts, on the other hand, are an indication of an obligation by
the school system to continue renewing your contract for as long
as you will accept it. These contracts are usually issued after
you have served the school system for a number of years and have
fulfilled the educational requirements required by the system to
reach a status of continuing contract. Although the terms "continuing" and "limited" are not universally accepted as the desig-

nations for such contracts within all school systems in the United States, you will everywhere find contracts which resemble them. When you accept a position, in almost every instance it will be on a limited contract basis. In order to develop job security you should inquire about the requirements for continuing contracts. Start the first year of your service working toward the objective of eventually gaining a continuing contract and tenure within a school system. The detailed rules and regulations for gaining such status are usually found in the Board of Education Policy Manual. Many of the suggestions in this book are directed toward your successful experience as a beginning teacher. Although the answers are not complete, this book should act as a traffic light, signaling when you should do further research into a situation and what situations are important for your success in the teaching profession. Whether you choose to heed this advice or not is your decision, but all of these items are important to your continuing success as a educator. Failure to understand the repercussions of these items can cost you valuable time and money in pursuing your profession.

GROOMING. Contrary to popular belief, grooming remains an important consideration when being interviewed for employment by a school system. How does poor grooming contribute to the possibility of you being passed up as a prospective teacher in a school system? General dress and appearance are always taken into account when interviewing a prospective teacher. Most school systems find themselves perpetuating the value system that has evolved in that particular community. Most smaller communities in the United States have a relatively conservative value structure. This does not mean that fashion and fads are outlawed in school systems. However, it does mean that dress must conform to the to the values of the individual school system where you are making application. In plain terms, most school administrators and Boards of Education frown upon blue jeans, long straggly unkempt hair, wild or exotic color combinations, excessively short dresses or excessively tight trousers, and other extremes of fashion. If you have difficulty rationalizing a change in your appearance to meet the requirements of a particular community's value system, consider it a role expectation. Remember you are being employed by the school system to perform a particular role, and that role requires that you maintain a certain standard appearance. This does not mean that you must believe in this appearance, it only indicates that failure to conform in this area may result in role conflict and thus jeopardize your teaching career. This is a very practical matter and it would seem that most prospective teachers would not have the problem. However, it has been my experience that this problem alone is responsible for the elimination of 50 per cent of the applicants for teaching positions.

Let commonsense be your guide with regard to hair style, fingernail care, teeth care, and general acceptable dress standards. A very sure key to direction in the area of grooming is the Board of Education dress code for students. If you find that the Board of Education has a very rigid dress code requiring students to conform in areas such as clothing and hair length, then you can assume that they will expect at least the same conformity from teachers. Once again, as you study a school system and consider the position for which you are applying, in the final analysis the decision is yours. However, to ignore the expectations of school systems and administrators completely shows political naivete and thus represents you poorly as a prospective teacher. The problem basically is not whether you agree or disagree with the expected dress code for teachers within a system; it is whether your salary justifies you adjusting your behavior to meet with the role expectations of the school system hiring you. If you can adjust your personality and behavioral patterns to meet with the expectations of the school system, thus limiting any conflict between what you desire your role to be and what the Board of Education desires, you will greatly improve your chances for success. It is much easier to influence change within a system if you are a part of it. Many systems measure a person's suggestions by the degree to which he has been successful working within its rules. For example, if you make a million dollars in our society, people will listen to what you have to say with regard to how to make money. Although this is a simplified explanation, a beginning teacher who accepts that this situation exists will greatly enhance his success. Although grooming is "old hat," remember you are being evaluated by recruiters who in most cases do not necessarily have the same value system as yourself. If you are going to be successful in your interview attempts, then practical common-sense behavior in these situations must prevail.

TEACHING ABROAD. Since I have spent three years in the foreign service working in Southeast Asia and the Middle East with teachers from all over the world, I include a paragraph explaining some of the advantages and disadvantages of overseas employment. Although opportunities in overseas employment are limited, I feel that for the adventurous beginning teacher this is an area that certainly should be considered. The advantages of teaching overseas are tremendous. It broadens the individual's perspective of his own society and enables him to enrich his contribution to his field through his foreign experiences. In general the following will explain briefly the types of personalities who should consider teaching assignments. An overseas teacher should be perceptive about his foreign counterparts. He should strive to understand how others feel about problems and occasionally put himself in their place. He should judge people by why they do things rather than by what they do and thus should be able to analyze the behavior of others and to project how they will act. He should strive to get suggestions from his peers and counterparts. He must accept local customs and avoid unconventional behavior within the society he is working. He should, of course, desire to be recognized as an authority in his field of specialization.

The ideal overseas teacher should respect the advantages of preplanning projects and systematically organizing the work at hand. His leadership qualities should be apparent in his behavioral actions. Tactfulness and logic should influence his judgments concerning arguments and disputes between others.

The ideal overseas teacher should be able to conform to new situations without criticizing the positions of authority. He must not become dependent upon the local people for sympathetic encouragement or allow them to become dependent upon him. Commonsense would dictate that he should never criticize or make fun of the local people, especially in public situations.

48

As you can see, although the above comments are directed basically toward overseas teaching positions, they are also universally true for all beginning teachers. It is my contention that if beginning teachers follow these common-sense rules, they will greatly enhance the potential of their success within a profession. Below are listed a few agencies which can help you in your search for an overseas teaching position.

1. The Digest of Executive Opportunities
   Box 815, New Canaan, Connecticut 06840

2. The Committee on International Exchange of Persons
   2101 Constitution Avenue, Washington, D. C. 20418

3. International Schools Services
   126 Alexander Street, Princton, New Jersey 08540

4. Overseas Laison Committee
   American Council on Education
   One DuPont Circle
   Washington, D. C. 20036

5. Overseas Personnel Office
   Gulf Oil Corporation
   P. O. Box 1166
   Pittsburgh, Pennsylvania 15230

6. Personnel Director
   Panama Canal Company
   Balboa Heights, Canal Zone

7. Dr. Harold E. Diets
   Professor of Education
   "Teaching Positions in Foreign Countries"
   Box 514
   Ames, Iowa 50010

EXPERIENCE: ADVANTAGE OR DISADVANTAGE. In the past experience in all cases has been considered an advantage when applying for a teaching position. Today this is not exactly true. You do not have to be an expert in education to realize that many school systems are in financial difficulty today. These financial crisis require that school systems review their spending. Since 80 per cent of a school system's cost are salaries, the common-sense solution is to hire young teachers without experience. These people come into the system at the low end of the salary schedule and thus staff the system at a reduced cost.

Today more than ever a beginning teacher has an advantage over the experienced teacher applying for a position in a new system. Many systems recruit primarily to reduce the overall cost of running their program. Thus, they recruit almost totally new, inexperienced teachers. Although this is an advantage for the teacher graduating from college, it is certainly a disadvantage for the experienced teacher trying to move or relocate from one school system to another.

In most cases school systems only hire experienced teachers where they have an unusual problem in a building. For example, if there are two or three problem classes within a given building, a recruiter might attempt to hire an experienced teacher to go into that building to provide stability to the classroom and organizational management for the building. It is my advice for the experienced teacher wishing to change school systems to follow the age-old method of relocating. Namely, first apply for substitute teaching within the new school system. When you apply for substitute teaching, also indicate to the personnel director your desire to be considered for a full-time position if such should occur. By doing this you establish yourself with the administrators and other teachers within the system and also have an opportunity to display your ability as an experienced teacher. Although nearly all teachers hired before the beginning of the school year are first-year teachers, this situation changes drastically after school actually starts. For example, if a personnel manager has an opening for an English teacher after the school year begins, it is difficult for him to locate first-year teacher and have him relocate immediately in the community in order to maintain classroom continuity for students during the change of teacher personnel. For this reason he will turn to his substitute book and seek out those experienced teachers who have proven themselves as substitutes and have indicated a desire to become full-time teachers within the system. At this point the experienced teacher's possibility for employment greatly increases because of the factors influencing the normal hiring procedure for beginning teachers.

It is my contention that experience can be both an advantage and a disadvantage when seeking a teaching position. If you are a first-year teacher, do not consider the fact that you have not had previous teaching experience a disadvantage. However, if you are an experienced teacher, try to follow the above process when applying for a teaching position in a new system. Although it may take more time for an experienced teacher actually to find a full-time position, I feel that the above process will yield positive results.